RRJC

first
animal
encyclopedia

Published 2013 by
A & C Black
an imprint of Bloomsbury Publishing Plc
50 Bedford Square, London, WC1B 3DP

www.bloomsbury.com

ISBN HB: 978-1-4088-4252-2

A CIP catalogue for this book is available from the British Library.

Picture acknowledgements:
Cover: All Shutterstock.
Insides: All Shutterstock aside from the following; p16 bottom left David
W. E. Hone, Helmut Tischlinger, Xing Xu, Fucheng Zhang/Wikimedia
Commons, p20 top right Anjwalker/Wikimedia Commons, p21 top right
markaharper1/Wikimedia Commons, p26-27 inset Nature Picture Library,
p32 bottom left Loren Javier/Flickr Creative Commons, p33 bottom left
petechar/Flickr Creative Commons, p37 top right Nature Picture Library,
p39 top right Nature Picture Library, p39 bottom right MidgleyDJ/
Wikimedia Commons, p48 bottom left P.E. Bragg/Wikimedia Commons,
p51 center left gailhampshire/Flickr Creative Commons, p59 top right
Nature Picture Library, p61 top right Jens Peterson/Wikimedia Commons.

Printed about bound in China by C&C Offset Printing Co., Ltd

1 3 5 7 9 10 8 6 4 2

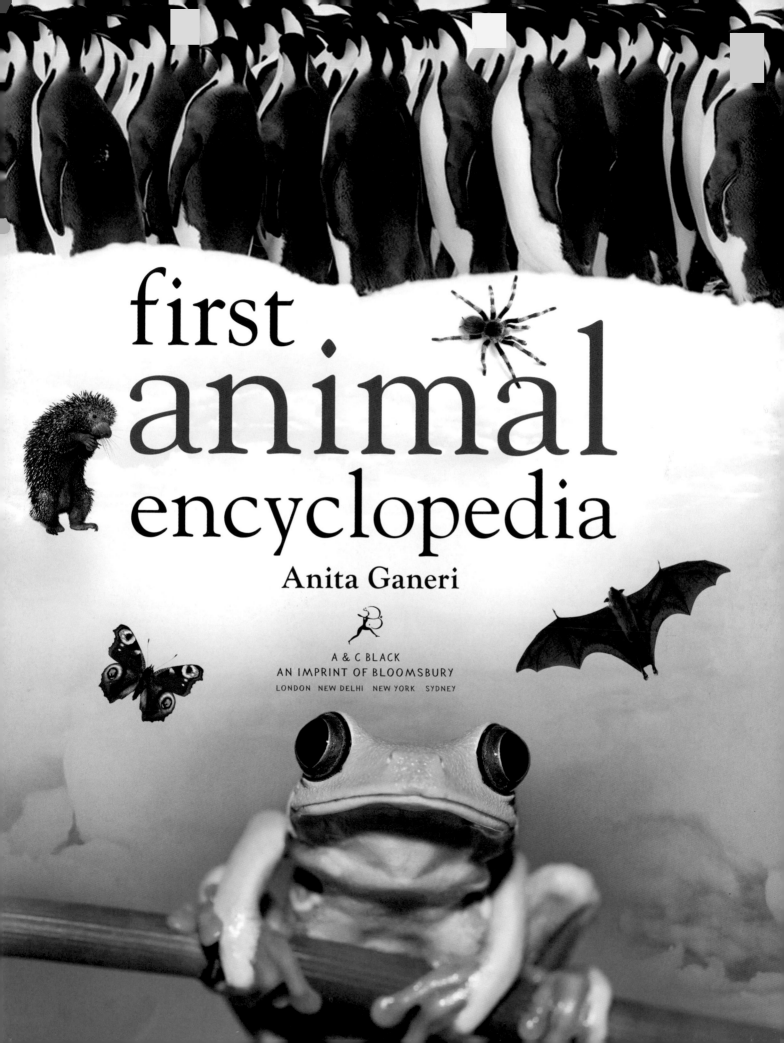

first animal encyclopedia

Anita Ganeri

A & C BLACK
AN IMPRINT OF BLOOMSBURY
LONDON NEW DELHI NEW YORK SYDNEY

Contents

Amazing animals

Animals are living things. Unlike plants, which can make the energy they need from the sun, animals need to find food to survive. Some animals eat plants; some eat other animals.

◄ Birds are animals with feathers, wings and beaks.

Animal groups

To make animals easier to study, scientists split them into groups. These groups are called: insects, arachnids, crustaceans, molluscs, fish, amphibians, reptiles, birds and mammals. All of the animals in a group have things in common. For example, all birds have beaks.

► Spiders are arachnids. They have eight legs.

◄ Snails, slugs and squid are molluscs.

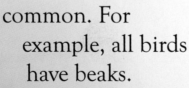

AWESOME!

No one knows how many different species, or kinds, of animals there are on Earth. Some scientists think there could be up to eight million.

▲ There are thousands of different types of fish.

▼ Tigers, lions and other big cats are mammals.

Animal bones

Fish, amphibians, reptiles, birds and mammals are called vertebrates. They have bony skeletons inside their bodies. Animals, such as insects, arachnids, molluscs and crustaceans are called invertebrates. They do not have bones inside their bodies. Instead, many of them have hard cases on the outside.

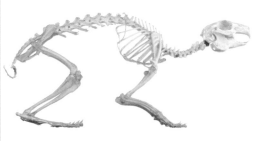

▲ Vertebrates have skeletons inside their bodies.

Warm or cold?

Some animals are warm-blooded. They can keep their bodies at the same temperature, whatever the weather outside. Others are cold-blooded. They rely on the weather to warm them up and cool them down.

Mammals

Mammals are warm-blooded animals. They all have some hair or fur on their bodies and breathe air. When mammals have babies, they look after them and feed them milk. Whales, tigers, wolves, gorillas and mice are all types of mammal, and so are you!

◀ Gorillas belong to a group of mammals called apes.

Rodents

Nearly half of all the mammals in the world are rodents, such as mice, rats, squirrels and porcupines. They all have four big front teeth. Rodents mostly eat seeds and plants. They live all over the world, apart from in icy Antarctica.

▼ Meerkats are social mammals that live in large groups – sometimes with up to 40 members.

► Orcas, or killer whales, are sea mammals.

Sea mammals

Whales, dolphins, seals and walruses are sea mammals. They spend their whole lives in or near the sea but still need to breathe air. Whales and dolphins come to the surface and breathe through a blowhole on the top of their heads.

► A bat's wings are also attached to its back legs.

Flying mammals

Some mammals are good gliders, but bats are the only mammals that can really fly. Their fingers are very long and have leathery skin stretched between them.

AWESOME!

Mammals are the only animals with earflaps around their ears, although not all mammals have these. The flaps help to send sounds down into their ears.

9

Little and large

Mammals come in many different shapes and sizes. From enormous whales to bee-sized bats, here are some of the biggest, smallest and tallest.

Record-breaker

The biggest mammal that has ever lived is the gigantic blue whale. It can grow to be more than 30 metres in length and weigh more than 20 African elephants.

▶ Giraffes have very long legs, and very long necks.

◀ Whales need water to hold their huge bodies up.

AWESOME!

Everything about a blue whale is massive! Even its huge tongue weighs around three tonnes - that's as heavy as 35 adult humans.

Tallest mammal

Giraffes are the tallest of all mammals, towering more than five metres above the ground. Giraffes use their long necks to reach juicy leaves high up in the trees.

Smallest mammals

Savi's pygmy shrew is so tiny that it can squeeze through earthworm tunnels in the ground. An adult shrew only weighs as much as a table tennis ball. Another miniature mammal is the bumblebee bat which is about the size of a large butterfly.

▲ This tiny shrew is one of the smallest mammals.

Largest on land

An adult male African elephant stands about three metres tall and weighs as much as eight cars. This makes it the largest mammal on land. It also has the biggest ears and the longest nose!

▶ A magnificent male African elephant.

Senses and communication

Mammals use their sharp senses to find food, keep out of danger, attract mates and guard their homes. All of these are vital skills for staying alive.

▼ You can smell a skunk 0.5 kilometres away.

Smelly skunk

To scare off an enemy, a skunk stamps its feet on the ground. If this doesn't work, it does a handstand, lifts up its tail and squirts out a liquid that smells terrible, like a mixture between rotten eggs and burning rubber.

Bat radar

Many bats hunt at night, using sound to find food and their way around. A bat makes lots of high squeaking sounds, which hit objects, such as insects. The sounds then send back echoes, which the bat picks up with its sharp ears. From these, it can tell what and where the object is.

AWESOME!

If a Virginia opossum is in danger, it falls on the ground and pretends to be dead until its attacker gives up and leaves it alone.

Noisy monkeys

Howler monkeys live in the South American rainforests. Every morning and evening, groups of monkeys howl to warn other monkeys away from their trees. The ear-splitting noise can be heard eight kilometres away.

◀ Howler monkeys have one of the loudest mammal voices.

▼ Male humpback whales sing to attract females.

Whale song

Whales send messages to each other by singing underwater. They have very loud but very low voices. Some humpback whale songs can last for half an hour and be heard hundreds of kilometres away.

13

Animals at the Poles

It is freezing cold and windy at the Poles. Ice covers large parts of the land and sea. Amazingly, many animals live at the Poles. They have special ways of keeping warm, dry and safe.

Polar bear

Polar bears live in the Arctic. They hunt for seals on the sea ice. To keep warm, they have thick fur and a layer of fat underneath their skin. Small bumps and long hairs on their feet help them to grip the slippery ice.

▲ An Arctic fox in summer (above) and winter (below).

Arctic fox

In summer, Arctic foxes grow a greyish-brown coat so they can hide from enemies among the rocks. In winter, they grow white coats so they can hide among the ice and snow.

◀ A polar bear hunts on the Arctic ice.

Penguins

Emperor penguins breed on the Antarctic ice in the middle of winter. The females lay their eggs, then go off to sea to feed. The males carry the eggs on their feet, covered by a flap of skin.

The Antarctic cod is a fish that lives in the icy sea around Antarctica. It has a special chemical, like *antifreeze* in its blood. This stops its body freezing solid.

▼ Male Emperor penguins huddle together for warmth.

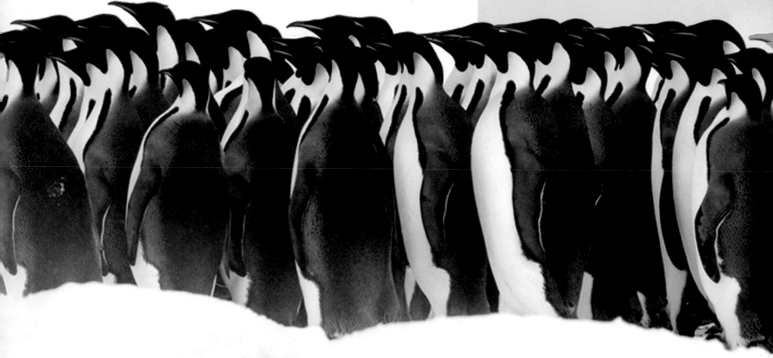

▼ Weddell seals have sharp teeth!

Seals

The Weddell seal lives in Antarctica. It dives underwater to feed on fish and squid. If the sea is frozen, the seal chews a hole in the ice with its sharp teeth. Then it can come up to the surface to breathe.

15

Birds

Birds have wings and bodies covered in feathers. They have beaks instead of jaws, and lay eggs with hard shells. Birds are warm-blooded, and live all over the world, even in Antarctica.

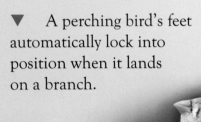

▼ A perching bird's feet automatically lock into position when it lands on a branch.

Perching birds

More than half of all the different kinds of birds are perching birds, such as robins, finches and wrens. They have special feet for gripping branches - three toes point forward and one points backwards. This means that a bird can sleep without falling off its perch.

AWESOME!

Many scientists think that birds are related to dinosaurs. They have found fossils of bird-like dinosaurs that had feathers and wings, and were able to fly.

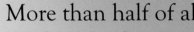

▶ Flamingos get their colour from the food they eat.

Birds of prey

With their sharp talons, hooked beaks, superb eyesight and powerful wings, birds of prey are built for hunting. Many, such as buzzards and eagles, spot their prey of rodents, fish and snakes, from the air. Then they swoop down and scoop it up with their feet.

▲ An eagle swooping down on its prey.

▼ Swans and other water birds have webbed feet for swimming.

Water birds

Many birds live near rivers, lakes and streams. Ducks, swans and geese have waterproof feathers and webbed feet for swimming. Flamingos have long legs for wading through the shallows. To feed, they stick their heads upside-down in the water and sieve out tiny shrimp with their beaks.

Nests and eggs

Lots of birds build nests as a safe, warm place to lay their eggs. Some nests are simple holes scraped into the ground while others are made from mud, sticks, reeds and branches, and take many weeks to build.

▲ Many birds build their nests up in trees, out of reach of hungry animals.

▼ Social weaver birds build their huge nests in the branches of trees. Sometimes the branches break under the weight.

AWESOME!

Ostriches lay the biggest eggs of any birds. Each egg can be as heavy as 25 hen's eggs. Vervain hummingbirds lay the smallest birds' eggs – about the size of peas!

Nest neighbours

Sociable weaver birds in Africa live together in an enormous nest. First, they make a giant roof from twigs in the tree tops. Underneath, they weave hundreds of smaller, grass nests. Each nest is lined with soft plants, cotton, fluff and fur. Sharp spikes of straw protect the nests from hungry baboons and snakes.

Hatching out

► The mother swan sits gently on her eggs.

1 A mute swan builds a large nest from plants on the riverbank.

2 The female lays four to eight eggs. She sits on them to keep them warm while the male guards the nest.

3 After about five weeks, the cygnets (baby swans) start breaking through their egg shells.

4 The cygnets are a brown-grey colour, with fluffy down. Later they grow brown feathers followed by white.

5 Cygnets can swim soon after hatching.

Up in the air

Most birds have bodies designed for flying. They have hollow, light bones and wings which they flap to stay up in the air.

Humming birds

Tiny hummingbirds can fly forwards, up, down and even backwards. They flap their wings so fast that they make a humming sound. Hummingbirds use their amazing flying skills to hover in front of flowers and feed on the sweet nectar inside.

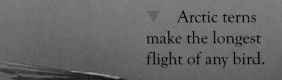

Arctic terns make the longest flight of any bird.

Long journey

Some birds make long journeys to find warm places to live and feed. The champion is the Arctic tern which flies non-stop for about eight months of the year. Each year, this little bird travels all the way from the Arctic to Antarctica, and back again.

A hummingbird hovering while it feeds.

A male Count Raggi's bird of paradise showing off his feathers.

Fabulous feathers

Birds use them for flying, keeping warm and attracting mates. The male Count Raggi's bird of paradise has long, bright red feathers on its back. To impress a female, he hangs upside down from a branch and shows them off.

Ostriches have the longest legs of any bird.

▼ Penguins can swim fast through the water.

Flightless birds

Not all birds can fly but they have other ways of getting about. Penguins are fast swimmers, using their wings as flippers. Ostriches are too heavy to fly but have long legs and can run very fast.

Mountains

▼ Mountain people keep yaks for their milk, meat and wool.

Mountains can be very cold and windy places. The mountain slopes are sometimes bare and rocky or covered in ice and snow meaning that only the toughest animals can survive in this harsh habitat.

High-rise yaks

Yaks live high up in the mountains of Asia. To protect them from the cold, they have long, thick, shaggy coats with two layers of hair for extra warmth.

▼ A lammergeier smashes open bones on a rock.

AWESOME!

Alpine marmots survive the winter by sleeping in underground burrows. They wake up again in spring, when it is warmer and there is more food about.

Bone-breakers

Lammergeiers live on mountains in Europe, Asia and Africa. They feed on dead animals' bones. To reach the juicy marrow inside, they drop the bones on to the rocks to smash them.

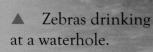

▲ Zebras drinking at a waterhole.

Grasslands

Grasslands are huge plains found around the world. They are too dry and dusty for many plants to grow there, apart from tough grasses and a few trees.

▼ An anteater can tear open an anthill with its strong claws.

Giant anteater

Giant anteaters from South America eat ants and termites which they slurp up with their long, sticky tongues. In just one day, they can eat up to 30,000 ants!

Huge herds

Huge herds of zebras, giraffes and antelopes graze on the grasslands in Africa. They have to keep a good look out for hungry hunters, such as lions, leopards and hyenas.

AWESOME!

Dung beetles lay their eggs in poo (dung). A beetle rolls some poo into a ball, then lays an egg in it. When the egg hatches, the grub has a ready meal of poo to eat.

Reptiles

Reptiles are cold-blooded and have scaly skin. Many live in hot places because they need sunshine to keep their bodies warm. Most reptiles lay eggs. Lizards, snakes, turtles, tortoises, crocodiles and alligators are all reptiles.

▲ Milk snakes mostly hunt rodents at night.

▲ Knob-tailed geckos have short bodies, big heads and knobbly tails.

Lizards

Lizards can be tiny geckos or huge komodo dragons. As they grow bigger, their old skins get too tight. They have new, bigger skins underneath.

Crocodiles and alligators

Crocodiles and alligators look very alike. They have armour-plated bodies, strong tails and massive jaws, filled with sharp, pointed teeth. They live in and near water.

Snakes

Snakes have long, thin bodies. Their shape is good for slithering, climbing, swimming and burrowing. The longest snake is the reticulated python from Southeast Asia. It grows as long as six bicycles.

▲ Turtles have feet like flippers for swimming.

▼ Giant tortoises live on the Galapagos Islands in South America.

Tortoises and turtles

Tortoises and turtles have strong, bony shells. Some of them can pull their heads and limbs inside their shells. Tortoises live on land but turtles spend most of their time in water.

▼ Elasmosaurus was a plesiosaur that lived in the prehistoric oceans.

AWESOME!

Dinosaurs and plesiosaurs were reptiles. They lived on Earth millions of years ago.

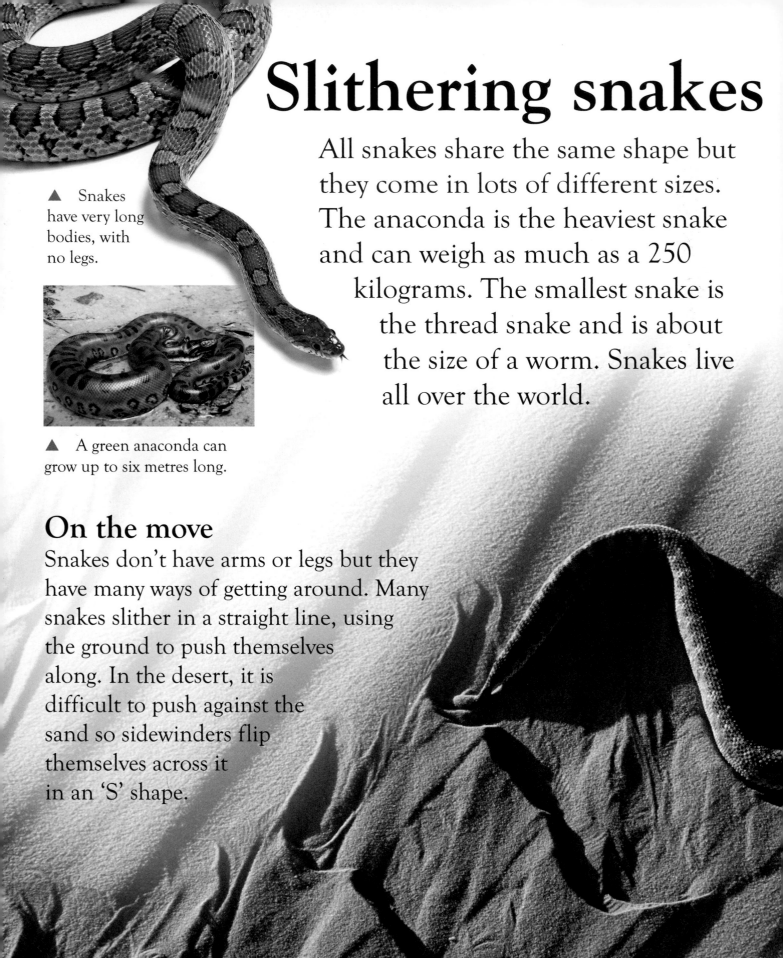

Slithering snakes

▲ Snakes have very long bodies, with no legs.

▲ A green anaconda can grow up to six metres long.

All snakes share the same shape but they come in lots of different sizes. The anaconda is the heaviest snake and can weigh as much as a 250 kilograms. The smallest snake is the thread snake and is about the size of a worm. Snakes live all over the world.

On the move

Snakes don't have arms or legs but they have many ways of getting around. Many snakes slither in a straight line, using the ground to push themselves along. In the desert, it is difficult to push against the sand so sidewinders flip themselves across it in an 'S' shape.

AWESOME!

As they grow bigger, snakes grow new, bigger skins. They rub against a rock or tree to loosen their old skin and then wriggle out.

► A baby snake hatching out of its egg.

Snake babies

Many snakes lay their eggs and then slither away. But the female python coils her body around her eggs to keep them warm and stays with them for several months until they hatch.

◄ A sidewinder flipping across the sand.

Self defence

Snakes have clever ways of protecting themselves from harm. Some snakes bite poison into their attackers with their long fangs. But the spitting cobra squirts poison into its enemy's face, which can blind it.

► A cobra can spit poison as far as two metres.

Food and feeding

Many reptiles are meat-eaters and use lots of different ways to catch their food. Some use fangs and poison to kill their prey while others use their strong jaws and sharp teeth. Some reptiles even squeeze their prey to death.

▼ Crocodiles eat fish, reptiles, monkeys and even zebra and wildebeest.

AWESOME!

A crocodile's eyes, ears and nostrils are on top of its head. This means that it can still see, hear and hunt for prey while hidden under the water.

Croc attack!

A crocodile lies at the water's edge, waiting for an animal to come by for a drink. It then bursts out of the water, grabs its victim in its massive jaws and drags it underwater to drown it.

A tight squeeze

Some snakes, like the boa constrictor, don't use poison to kill their food. Instead they wrap their body around their prey and squeeze until the animal suffocates to death. Then it swallows it whole. Snakes have such stretchy jaws that they can eat animals as large as crocodiles.

▲ A snake swallowing a lizard.

Sticky tongue

A chameleon mostly eats insects and spiders. It sits on a branch, then, suddenly, shoots out its enormous tongue. Its sticky tongue is as long as its body.

▼ A chameleon uses its big eyes to watch for prey.

Deserts

Deserts are the driest places on Earth and can be baking hot in the daytime. This means animals that live in deserts have to keep cool and find enough water to stay alive.

Cool camels

Camels can go for days without finding food or water and live off fat stored in their humps. They also save water by doing very dry poos. Camels have two sets of eyelashes and can close their nostrils which helps keep sand out.

◀ A fennec fox's huge ears help to keep it cool.

Big ears

Fennec foxes, found in the Sahara Desert, have huge ears for listening out for prey. Their ears also give off heat, which helps to keep the foxes cool.

Spadefoot toads

In very dry weather, spadefoot toads from North America sleep in cool, damp burrows underground and stay there for many months until it rains again. They then quickly find the nearest pond to lay their eggs.

▲ Spadefoot toads get their name from their feet which they use for digging.

Drinking fog

This small black beetle from the Namib Desert drinks fog that rolls in from the sea! At night, it stands on a sand dune with its head down and its body sticking up into the air. Tiny drops of fog collect on its back, which then trickle into its mouth.

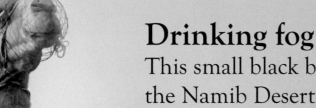

◄ Fog-drinking beetles in the Namib Desert.

◄ Camels are well suited to desert life.

AWESOME!

A Cape ground squirrel from Africa uses its big, bushy tail to provide shade from the sun.

Amphibians

Amphibians are cold-blooded animals. They have smooth, damp skin that helps them to breathe. Amphibians are at home in water and on land. Many live on land as adults, but have to be in the water to lay their eggs.

◀ Amphibians, like this newt, live in water and on land.

AWESOME!

The biggest amphibian in the world is the Chinese giant salamander. It can grow as long as a bed. It lives in mountain streams and eats fish, shrimp and insects.

▲ Tree frogs have sticky toes for climbing trees.

Frogs and toads

Frogs and toads have short bodies, damp skin and no tails. Frogs have smooth skin and long legs for jumping, while toads have shorter legs for walking, and bumpier skin. The biggest frog, a goliath frog, is as big as a cat. The smallest frog could sit on your fingertip.

▼ Newts lay their eggs in the water.

▲ This salamander's colourful skin is poisonous.

Newts and salamanders

Newts and salamanders look like lizards, with long bodies, short tails and long legs. They are meat-eaters, feeding on worms, slugs and insects. Some, like the fire salamander, have brightly-coloured skins. This warns hungry enemies that they are poisonous to eat.

▲ Newts breathe through their damp skin.

Caecilians

With long, thin bodies and no legs, caecilians look like worms. They only live in warm places, where they burrow in damp soil and mud. They eat insects and other worms that they find by smell. They use their heads as spades for digging up their prey.

Egg to frog

Frogs start life as tiny eggs that hatch into fish-like tadpoles. Slowly, the tadpoles change shape and turn into little froglets that look like the parent frogs.

1 In spring, an adult frog lays thousands of jelly-like eggs in the water. The eggs are called frogspawn.

2 After about 10 days, tadpoles hatch from the eggs. They look like fish with long tails for swimming.

▶ A tiny tadpole grows inside each egg.

3 The tadpoles lose their tails and grow legs. They look more like tiny frogs.

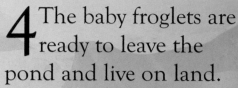 **The baby froglets are ready to leave the pond and live on land.**

▶ The adult frog likes to live in damp places.

◀ A male midwife toad takes care of his eggs.

Caring dads

Some amphibians have strange ways of looking after their eggs. A male Darwin's frog keeps his tadpoles in his mouth. When they turn into froglets, he spits them out. A male midwife toad winds the eggs around his back legs. He carries them until they are ready to hatch.

AWESOME!

Some adult amphibians only live for a few months. But a Japanese giant salamander reached the age of 55 years old.

Staying safe

Amphibians mostly eat insects, worms, slugs and snails. But they also make tasty meals for other animals, including other amphibians. They have clever ways of keeping out of danger - hopping, hiding and using poison.

▲ Fire salamanders have poisonous skin.

AWESOME!

If a spiny newt is caught by an enemy, it sticks its long, sharp ribs out through its skin and stabs poison into its attacker.

Hiding away

Many amphibians are brown, grey or green. This helps them to hide from their enemies. The Asian horned frog has a brilliant disguise. It looks just like a dead leaf. Its body is flat and brown, and it has leaf-shaped 'horns' above its eyes.

Leap frog

Frogs have long, strong back legs for leaping away from danger. A frog's legs are folded up until it's time to jump. Then it straightens its legs and pushes off from the ground.

The South African sharp-nosed frog can leap more than five metres in a single hop – that's about 90 times its own body length.

In nature, bright colours are often a warning.

Poison dart frog

Poison dart frogs look pretty but their bright colours aren't just for show. They warn hungry enemies that the frogs are deadly poisonous to eat. The golden poison dart frog has enough poison in their skin to kill ten humans.

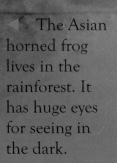

The Asian horned frog lives in the rainforest. It has huge eyes for seeing in the dark.

River and lake animals

Rivers and lakes are home to many different animals. Animals find food and shelter in or near the water while fish swim and feed underwater. Birds nest in the plants by the water's edge as dragonflies swoop down on insects to eat.

Fierce fish

Piranhas are small fish that swim in rivers in South America. They are famous for their razor-sharp, triangular teeth and for snapping up their prey. But not all piranhas are fierce meat-eaters. Some feed on fruits and seeds that fall into the water.

▲ Piranhas hunt in large groups, called shoals.

▶ Otters are sleek and streamlined for swimming.

Sleek otters

Otters have sleek bodies and webbed feet for swimming. They use their long tails to steer in the water. Their fur is thick and waterproof which keeps them warm and dry. Otters mainly feed on fish but also eat birds and frogs.

▶ An archer fish shooting down its prey.

Caring cichlids

Cichlids are unusual fish that live in lakes in East Africa. The female lays her eggs and then scoops them up into her mouth to keep them safe. When the eggs hatch, the baby fish stay inside their mother's mouth for another few days before swimming away.

▼ Cichlids are fish that look after their young.

▲ A mouth brooder holds its eggs in its mouth.

Fish

Fish are cold-blooded animals. They live in fresh and salty water, in seas, rivers, streams and lakes. Most fish have bodies covered in scales, with fins to help them swim. They breathe oxygen from the water they live in.

▲ Sharks have bendy skeletons.

Bony fish

Most fish have bony skeletons inside their bodies. The biggest bony fish is the sunfish. Adults can grow to the size of cars but they start off as eggs only as big as pinheads. The longest bony fish is the oarfish, which can grow to be more than three metres long.

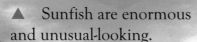
▲ Sunfish are enormous and unusual-looking.

Sharks and rays

Sharks, rays and skates don't have hard bones. Instead, their skeletons are made from soft, rubbery cartilage. It is just like the bendy cartilage in your nose and ears. You can read more about sharks on pages 44-45.

Jawless fish

Hagfish and lamphreys have long bodies but no scales. They do not have jaws for eating. Instead, they have sharp teeth and funnel-like mouths for sucking up food.

▲ Lampreys cling on to fish with their mouths and start to feed.

AWESOME!

Mudskipppers are unusual fish that can live out of the water because they can breathe air. They use their fins as elbows to skip about on the mud.

▲ Rays seem to fly through the water on wing-like fins.

41

All shapes and sizes

Most fish have strong, streamlined bodies for swimming. They have fins on their backs, sides and tails which they use for pushing their bodies through the water, turning, balancing and steering. However, not all fish are a typical fishy shape!

▲ This fish has a normal, fish-shaped body.

▼ The fish's body flattens out.

Flat fish

Flat fish, such as turbot and plaice, start off as normal-shaped fish. But gradually, one eye moves round to the other side of the head, and their bodies flatten out. Most flatfish live on the seabed.

▶ The fish lies on the sea bed.

Seahorses

Seahorses are bony fish, despite their strange shape. They have upright bodies and long snouts for sucking up food. They are not very strong swimmers but curl their long tails around plants or coral to keep themselves from being swept away.

◄ Seahorses are slow, weak swimmers.

Gone fishing

An angler fish has a huge mouth, lined with sharp teeth, and a long, thin fin growing over its head. At the end of the fin is a blob of light that attracts small fish. When the fish gets close enough, the angler gobbles it up.

► Angler fish live in the deep sea where food is hard to find.

Super sharks

Sharks are the most famous fish in the sea. There are hundreds of different kinds. Some are sleek hunters that speed through the water looking for food. Others are gentle giants who feed on tiny sea creatures.

A shark on the hunt for food.

Whale shark

The biggest shark is the gigantic whale shark. It can grow up to 18 metres long. It swims along with its massive mouth open, sucking in water. Then it pushes the water out and swallows the tiny sea animals left behind.

Whale sharks are huge but harmless.

Killer shark

The great white shark is a fierce hunter and meat eater. Using its jagged, razor-sharp teeth, it catches fish, seals, sea lions and dolphins. This shark never runs out of teeth. When the old ones fall out, new ones grow to take their place.

▲ A great white shark's fearsome mouth.

▼ A hammerhead has a flat, hammer-shaped head.

Hammer head

The hammerhead shark has a hammer-shaped head, with eyes at each end. As it swims, it moves its head from side to side so that it can look all around for prey. Its favourite food is stingray, but it also eats squid, fish and even other hammerhead sharks.

Coral reef animals

Coral reefs are made by tiny sea animals, called coral polyps. They build hard cases around their bodies. When they die, the cases are left behind. Reefs provide plenty of food and shelter for thousands of amazing animals.

Reef fish

Thousands of fish live on coral reefs. Many, such as the butterfly fish, swim in large groups, called shoals. This helps to keep them safe from enemies who find a group hard to attack. Butterfly fish are brightly coloured which helps them to tell each other apart.

▼ Many reef fish are brightly coloured with strong patterns.

Keeping clean
Small fish, called wrasse, help keep other reef fish clean. Fish as big as moray eels stay still while the wrasse pick dead skin and dirt off them. The eels even let the wrasse into their mouths to clean bits of food from their sharp teeth!

▲ A wrasse cleaning the skin of a moray eel.

AWESOME!

Giant clams are the biggest shells in the world. They can measure more than one metre wide and weigh a quarter of a tonne. They live in the Pacific and Indian Oceans.

▲ A sleeping bag takes about 30 minutes to make.

Sleeping bags
Parrot fish get their name from their sharp, beak-like teeth. During the day, they feed on coral. At night, they keep themselves safe by making jelly-like bubbles around their bodies, like fishy sleeping bags.

47

Insects

Insects are easy to tell apart from other animals. They have six legs and many have wings. Their bodies are divided into three parts - the head, the thorax and the abdomen. Insects live all over the world. There are at least a million kinds of insects and probably many more.

▲ Insects have antennae on their heads which they use for touching and smelling.

▲ Stag beetle

▲ Meal beetle

▲ Rhinoceros beetle

AWESOME!

The longest insect in the world is a giant stick insect from Borneo. It lives in the rainforest and can grow as long as your arm.

Beetles

One in three insects are beetles. They range from animals bigger than your hand to those only the size of dots. Beetles look as if they are wearing armour. Their front wings are hard and thick. They cover and protect the beetles' back wings.

Butterflies and moths

To tell butterflies and moths apart, look at their antennae (feelers). Butterflies have club-shaped antennae while a moths' antennae are plain or feathery. Most butterflies come out during the day whereas most moths come out at night.

▲ Can you tell this moth and butterfly apart?

Ants and termites

Tiny ants and termites live in huge colonies (groups). The queen is head of the colony. There are also workers who find food, build nests and keep guard. Termites build huge towers to live in out of earth and spit. Some towers can stand twice as tall as a person!

▼ These huge towers were built by millions of termites.

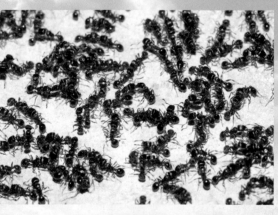

◄ Ants are incredibly strong for their size.

◄ Termites are tiny insects.

Birth of a butterfly

Many insects go through amazing changes as they grow up and turn into adults. Butterflies start life as tiny eggs and hatch into caterpillars which transform into beautiful butterflies.

1 A female butterfly lays her eggs on a leaf in the spring. She can lay up to 100 eggs in a day.

▼ Tiny caterpillars hatching out of eggs.

2 About a week later, the eggs start to hatch. A tiny caterpillar crawls out of each egg.

▲ Caterpillars have big appetites.

3 For the next three weeks, the caterpillars feed on the leaves and grow bigger.

4 Next, the caterpillar hangs upside down from a leaf and forms a hard case around its body.

5 Inside, the caterpillar's body completely changes and becomes a butterfly.

6 After about 12 days, the case splits open and the butterfly pulls itself out.

▼ Unlike many insects, female earwigs guard their eggs carefully.

▲ The butterfly holds its wings out to dry in the sun.

Earwig nursery

Female earwigs look after their eggs carefully. A female digs a hole in the ground where she lays her eggs. She sits over them to protect them, turning them over from time to time to keep them clean. When the eggs hatch, she carries on guarding them for a week or two.

AWESOME!

Caterpillars are big eaters but the caterpillar of the polyphemus moth is the greediest. In the first few months of its life, it eats about 86,000 times its own weight in leaves.

On the move

Insects have many ways of moving about to find food, mates, and escape from enemies. They can fly, run, wriggle, jump, dive, swim, and even walk on water without sinking.

Hunter on wings

Dragonflies have long, slender bodies and two pairs of wings. They are superb fliers. Emperor dragonflies can zoom through the air at speeds of up to 38 kilometres per hour. They use their flying skills to catch and eat butterflies and other insects in the air.

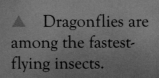

▲ Dragonflies are among the fastest-flying insects.

▼ Pond skaters skating across the surface of the water.

Pond skating

Pond skaters are little bugs that walk on the surface of the water. They have long, thin legs to spread their weight and waxy pads on their feet to stop them sinking. They skate across the water, looking for tiny insects to eat.

Speedy cockroach

The American cockroach is probably the fastest running insect. To match it, a human sprinter would have to race along at an astonishing 330 kilometres per hour!

▲ Cockroaches can live almost anywhere and eat almost anything!

AWESOME!

For their size, fleas are amazing jumpers. They can jump about 160 times their own height, and can keep jumping non-stop for hours or even days on end!

► A monarch butterfly feeding.

Long-distance

Every autumn, millions of monarch butterflies fly from cold Canada to the warmth of California and Mexico. Some fly more than 3,000 kilometres. In the spring, some of the butterflies fly back north again.

Rainforest animals

Tropical rainforests grow around the equator where it is hot and rainy all year round. They are home to millions of animals - more than anywhere else on Earth. Animals find plenty of food to eat and places to shelter among the rainforest trees and plants.

▼ Jaguars have strong jaws and sharp teeth.

Jungle hunter

Jaguars are skilful hunters, stalking their food such as deer and tapirs. Their spotted coats hide them among the trees. Then they pounce and kill their prey with a single bite. Their teeth are so sharp that they can even crack open hard turtle shells.

▲ Is it an insect or is it a flower?

Deadly disguise

The orchid mantis has a deadly disguise. It is the same colour as the flower it sits on, and its wings and legs look like petals. Perfectly hidden, it waits for small insects to visit. Then it grabs them and gobbles them up.

AWESOME!

Leaf-cutter ants are tiny but incredibly strong. They can lift 50 times their own body weight in leaves.

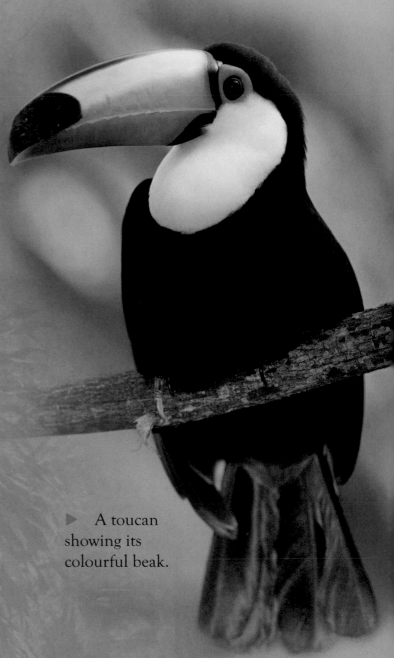

▶ A toucan showing its colourful beak.

Bright bills

Toucans are famous for their long, brightly coloured bills. They use them for picking fruit that other birds cannot reach. Once a toucan has picked a fruit, it tosses its head back and swallows its snack whole.

Arachnids

Spiders, scorpions, ticks and mites belong to a group of animals, called arachnids. They usually have eight legs, and bodies divided into two parts.

Spiders

Many spiders spin webs, using silk that they make in their bodies. They use their webs to catch insects to eat. The biggest webs are made by golden orb-web spiders in India. These webs are as big as a bed sheet, stretched out between trees.

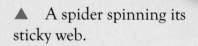

▲ A spider spinning its sticky web.

Scorpions

Like spiders, scorpions have eight legs but they also have two large pincers and a long, curved tail with a poisonous sting at the end. Scorpions use their stings to kill their prey and to protect themselves from attack.

▶ Mites are tiny but they share the same body plan as spiders and scorpions.

Mites and ticks

Mites and ticks are tiny. Most mites are the size of a grain of salt but they can cause problems. Dust mites live in people's houses, feeding on flakes of human skin. They get into mattresses and bedding, and some people are allergic to them. Ticks are blood-suckers. Some feed on blood from animals and spread diseases.

AWESOME!

The biggest spider in the world is the goliath bird-eating spider from the South American rainforests. It has a big, hairy body with long, hairy legs and is the size of a dinner plate!

◀ Some scorpions are deadly poisonous.

Crustaceans

Crustaceans have soft bodies, covered in hard shells. They have legs that bend at joints, and two pairs of feelers on their heads. Many have their eyes on stalks. Lobsters, crabs, shrimp and barnacles are all kinds of crustaceans.

▲ A crab's hard shell protects its soft body.

Follow my lobster

Spiny lobsters usually live in cracks in rocks and coral reefs. Each year, thousands of them travel many kilometres to warmer water. They walk along in lines, using their claws to hold on to the lobster in front. Each line can be more than 50 lobsters long.

▼ Spiny lobsters feed on crabs, clams, sea urchins and snails.

▶ Adult krill grow to about 1-2 centimetres long.

Whale food

Krill are crustaceans that look like tiny shrimp. In the Southern Ocean, they live in huge groups many metres deep. Krill are eaten by many animals, including fish, penguins, seals and whales. Blue whales can eat four tonnes of krill a day.

Hold tight

Young barnacles look like tiny crabs, swimming in the water. Adults glue themselves on to a hard surface, such as a rock, whale or ship. They grow hard cases around their bodies and never move again. Their feathery legs wave about in the water to collect food.

AWESOME!

Woodlice look like insects but they are actually crustaceans that live on land. They live in dark, damp places, under logs or stones, and eat rotting leaves and plants.

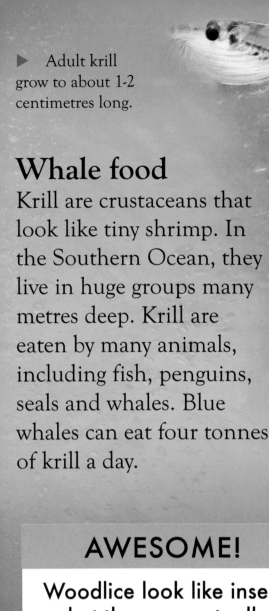

▷ Barnacles on a whale's head.

Molluscs

Molluscs come in a huge number of body shapes and sizes, from tiny seashells to gigantic squid. Slugs, snails, clams, limpets, octopus and cuttlefish are all kinds of molluscs.

▲ A snail uses its tentacles for smelling.

▲ A snail can curl up inside its shell.

Slugs and snails

Slugs and snails have slimy bodies and tentacles. They crawl across the ground, using a sucker-like foot under their bodies. Snails have shells around their soft bodies to protect them from harm. Slugs and sea slugs do not have shells.

◀ A shell with one part.

▼ These shells have two parts, joined by a hinge.

▼ Shells often wash up on beaches.

Sorts of shells

Many molluscs live in the sea. You can find their shells washed up on the beach. Some, such as cowries, conches and cone shells, have one shell. Others, such as clams, scallops and cockles, have two. These are joined together with a hinge so that they can open and close.

▲ Squid kill their prey with a bite from their beaks.

Touch tentacles

Squid and octopus have large bodies and long tentacles. Squid are torpedo-shaped for fast swimming. They use their tentacles to grab crabs, lobsters and fish. Octopuses have beak-like mouths and a poisonous bite for catching food. They have very good eyesight for searching out food.

◀ Octopuses can swim and crawl over rocks.

63

Glossary

Abdomen The end part of an insect's body, behind the thorax.

Allergic If you are allergic to something, it can make you ill or make you cough, sneeze or itch.

Amphibians Animals, such as frogs and toads. They have smooth, damp skin and lay their eggs in the water.

Antennae Feelers on an animal's head that help it to touch and sense things around it.

Antifreeze A special liquid that stops other liquids from freezing.

Arachnids Animals, such as spiders and scorpions. They have eight legs and two parts of their bodies.

Birds Animals, such as ostriches and parrots. They have wings, feathers and beaks.

Breed Have babies.

Cartilage A soft, firm material that makes up the skeletons of sharks and rays.

Cold-blooded Animals that cannot control their own body temperature but rely on their surroundings to warm them up or cool them down.

Colonies Large groups of animals, such as termites.

Crustaceans Animals, such as lobsters and shrimp. They have soft bodies, covered in hard shells.

Down A covering of soft, fluffy feathers on baby birds.

Fangs Long, hollow teeth that snakes and some other animals use to inject poison into their prey.

Fish Animals, such as sharks and seahorses. They have fins and many have scaly bodies.

Frogspawn Jelly-like eggs laid by frogs in the water.

Glide Fly without flapping wings.

Graze Feed on grass and other plants.

Hollow Objects that are empty inside.

Hover When a bird stays still in the air by flapping its wings very quickly.

Insects Animals, such as beetles and flies. They have six legs and three parts to their bodies.

Invertebrates Animals without backbones or skeletons inside their bodies.

Mammals Mammals, such as tigers and kangaroos. They have hair or fur and feed their babies on milk.

Marrow Soft filling inside some bones.

Molluscs Animals, such as snails, clams and octopuses.

Oxygen A type of gas that animals need to breathe to stay alive.

Prey Animals that are hunted and eaten by other animals.

Reptiles Animals, such as crocodiles and snakes. They have scaly skin and lay eggs with soft shells.

Scales Small, overlapping flaps that grow from the skin of fish and some other animals.

Species A group of living things that have similar features.

Streamlined Having a long, sleek body that is good for cutting through water or air.

Talons Sharp claws on the feet of birds of prey.

Tentacles Long, bendy, arm-like parts of an animal's body. They are used for touching and gripping.

Thorax The part of an insect's body between its head and abdomen.

Vertebrates Animals with backbones and skeletons inside their bodies.

Warm-blooded Animals that can control their own body temperature so it stays the same, whatever the weather outside.

Webbed Feet that have skin stretched between the toes.

Index

Further Information

BOOKS

Animals on the Edge – Penguin
By Anna Claybourne (A & C Black, 2012)
Also included in the series: Hippo, Elephant, Rhino, Gorilla, Tiger.

Wild Animals (Horrible Geography Handbooks)
By Anita Ganeri (Scholastic, 2011)

Car-Sized Crabs and other Animal Giants
By Anna Claybourne (A & C Black, 2013)

Record Breakers: Astonishing Animals
By Anita Ganeri (Templar Publishing, 2013)

ONLINE RESOURCES

National Geographic – Kids Dare to Explore!
http://kids.nationalgeographic.co.uk/kids/

BBC Nature Wildlife
http://www.bbc.co.uk/nature/animals/

Arkive
www.arkive.org

ZSL
http://www.zsl.org